Jobs In My Community

by Barbara L. Luciano

PEARSON

Scott
Foresman

Editorial Offices: Glenview, Illinois • Parsippany, New Jersey • New York, New York
Sales Offices: Needham, Massachusetts • Duluth, Georgia • Glenview, Illinois
Coppell, Texas • Sacramento, California • Mesa, Arizona

We do many interesting kinds of work. Come and see what we do!

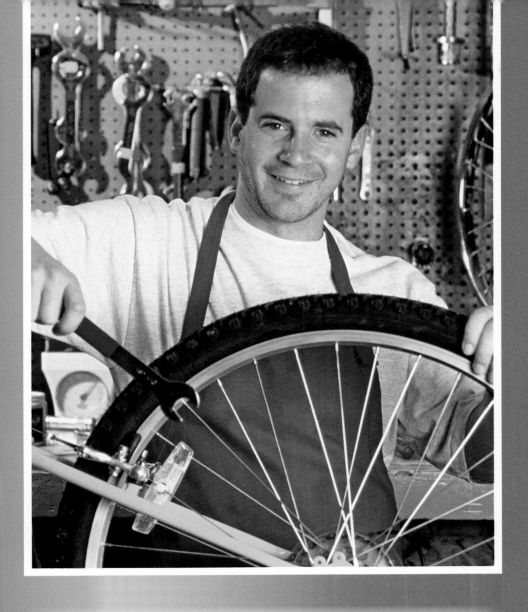

I work in a bicycle store.
I fix bicycles.

I make it safe near your school.
I am a police officer.

I sell all kinds of clothing.
I help people choose what to buy.

I work in an office.
I use a computer.

When you grow up, what job would you like to do?

Glossary

clothing what people wear

job something that needs to
be done

work what someone makes
or does

Write to It!

Draw a picture of yourself doing a job you might like to do when you are grown up. Write one sentence about the job.

Use another sheet of paper.

Fun Facts

- A bicycle has two wheels. A tricycle has three, and a unicycle has one.

- Some malls have thousands of sales clerks and security guards.

- An abacus was used to do math before computers were invented.

Genre	Comprehension Skill	Text Feature
Nonfiction	Compare and Contrast	Glossary

Scott Foresman Social Studies

PEARSON

Scott Foresman

scottforesman.com

ISBN 0-328-14779-6

90000

9 780328 147793

THE ROAD IS OPEN

A NOVEL

MICHAEL BURNS HAGGERTY